MIND BLOWING! THE BRAIN

MOVEMENT AND BALANCE

by Joyce Markovics

CHERRY LAKE PRESS
Ann Arbor, Michigan

CHERRY LAKE PRESS

Published in the United States of America by Cherry Lake Publishing Group
Ann Arbor, Michigan
www.cherrylakepublishing.com

Reading Adviser: Beth Walker Gambro, MS Ed., Reading Consultant, Yorkville, IL
Content Adviser: Mark W. Green, MD, Neurologist
Book Designer: Ed Morgan

Photo Credits: © freepik.com, cover and title page; © freepik.com, TOC; © Imaginechina Limited/Alamy Stock Photo, 4–5; © Jolygon/Shutterstock, 6; © freepik.com, 7; © freepik.com, 8; © freepik.com, 9; © freepik.com, 10; © freepik.com, 11; © Bangkoker/Shutterstock, 12; © freepik.com, 13; © freepik.com, 14; © freepik.com, 15; © freepik.com, 16; © freepik.com, 17 top; Henning Horn, Brian Burke, and Colin Stewart, Institute of Medical Biology, Agency for Science, Technology, and Research, Singapore, 17 bottom; © freepik.com, 18; © freepik.com, 19; © freepik.com, 20; © freepik.com, 21; © Fab_1/Shutterstock.com, 22.

Cherry Lake Press is an imprint of Cherry Lake Publishing Group.

Library of Congress Cataloging-in-Publication Data

Names: Markovics, Joyce L., author.
Title: Movement and balance / by Joyce Markovics.
Description: Ann Arbor, Michigan : Cherry Lake Publishing, [2022] | Series:
  Mind blowing! the brain | Includes bibliographical references and index.
  | Audience: Grades 4-6
Identifiers: LCCN 2021035325 (print) | LCCN 2021035326 (ebook) | ISBN
  9781534199569 (hardcover) | ISBN 9781668900703 (paperback) | ISBN
  9781668906460 (ebook) | ISBN 9781668902141 (pdf)
Subjects: LCSH: Motion—Juvenile literature. | Force and energy—Juvenile
  literature. | Equilibrium—Juvenile literature.
Classification: LCC QC127.4 .M37 2022 (print) | LCC QC127.4 (ebook) | DDC
  612.7/9—dc23
LC record available at https://lccn.loc.gov/2021035325
LC ebook record available at https://lccn.loc.gov/2021035326

Printed in the United States of America
Corporate Graphics

CONTENTS

HiGH-WiRE WALK

Viewers watched the cloudy sky and gasped. It was July 2013 in Kunming City, China. Above them, Aisikaier Wubulikaisimu balanced on a 2-inch (5-centimeter) wide beam that was 108 feet (33 meters) above the ground. Even more amazing was that the beam was strung between two rainbow-colored hot-air balloons.

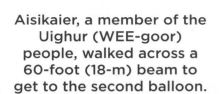

Aisikaier, a member of the Uighur (WEE-goor) people, walked across a 60-foot (18-m) beam to get to the second balloon.

Aisikaier walked quickly from one bobbing balloon to the other. At one point, the wind gusted, and he squatted to keep his balance. Onlookers froze with excitement. Aisikaier regained his balance, stood up, and kept walking. When he reached the second balloon, people cheered wildly. He had done it!

Aisikaier Wubulikaisimu broke a world record for fastest high-wire walk that day. He completed the challenge in just 38.35 seconds. Aisikaier would not have been able to do this balancing feat without one astonishing organ—his brain!

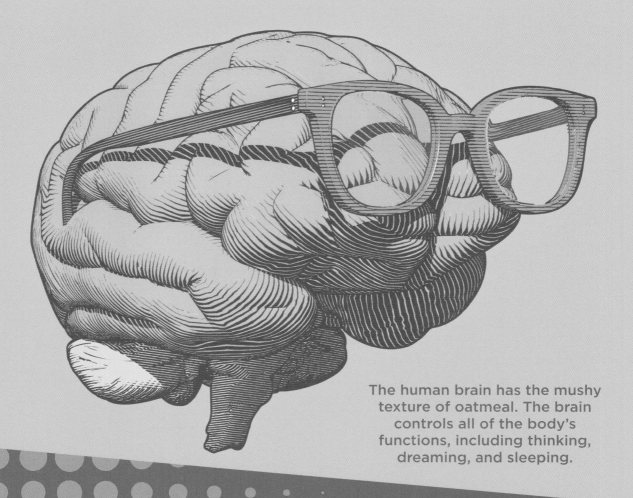

The human brain has the mushy texture of oatmeal. The brain controls all of the body's functions, including thinking, dreaming, and sleeping.

The brain is the control center for everything you do, including balance and movement. This wrinkly 3-pound (1.4-kilogram) organ makes it possible to stand on one foot, skip, or do a cartwheel. Every second, your brain takes in information from the world around you. Then it plans and carries out every single movement you make, while also keeping you balanced!

Balance is the ability to remain steady. It keeps you from falling over—no matter what position you're in.

BRAIN TOUR

Your brain is made up of a network of hundreds of billions of tiny cells called neurons (NOO-ronz). These neurons outnumber the stars in the Milky Way! Each neuron carries chemical and electrical signals across your brain and body. Neurons connect with other neurons using links called synapses.

Neurons have long arms called axons and shorter, branching arms known as dendrites.

Synapses make it possible for you to do everything—from forming a thought to riding a bike. Think about the first time you rode a bike. Was it easy? After you practiced, did riding get a lot easier? That's because when you do something over and over, your synapses strengthen.

Once your brain knows how to do something, such as ride a bike, you don't need to think about how to do it again.

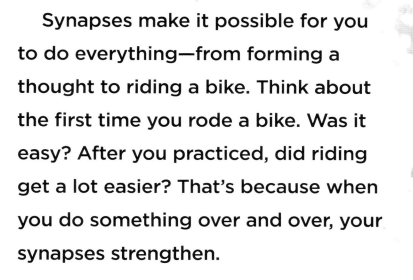

Your brain creates trillions of synapses until you're around 10 years old. After that, it gets rid of ones you don't use often. Use it or lose it!

The brain is part of the nervous system. This network of neurons and **nerves** sends signals zooming around your body. Signals travel along your spinal cord, which is the main nerve pathway between your brain and body. Smaller nerves branch out from your spinal cord to reach your whole body—all the way to your pinky toes!

In order to move your body, you use different parts of your brain. All of these parts work together like players on a sports team. The three main parts are the **cerebrum**, **cerebellum**, and **brain stem**.

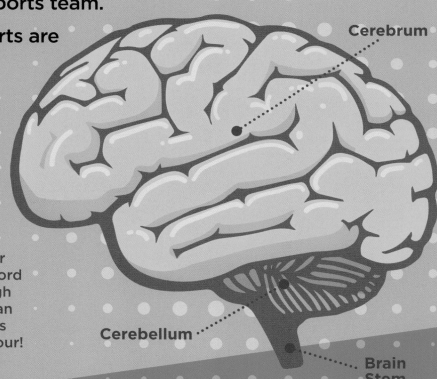

Cerebrum

Cerebellum

Brain Stem

Signals between your brain and your spinal cord zip around at very high speeds. The signals can travel up to 250 miles (402 kilometers) per hour!

Your spinal cord is a thick bundle of nerves that extends from your brain down your back. It's about 18 inches (46 centimeters) long and 0.5 inch (1.3 cm) thick like a rope. The backbone protects the spinal cord.

The cerebrum fills most of your skull. It's covered in pinkish-gray folds. It contains a lot of information that makes you who you are. For example, it's where memory, language, and the ability to feel and move are located. The cerebrum is divided into two halves and linked by a thick band of nerves in the middle.

The corpus callosum (KAWR-puhs kah-LOH-suhm) is the thick band of nerves that connects the two halves of the brain.

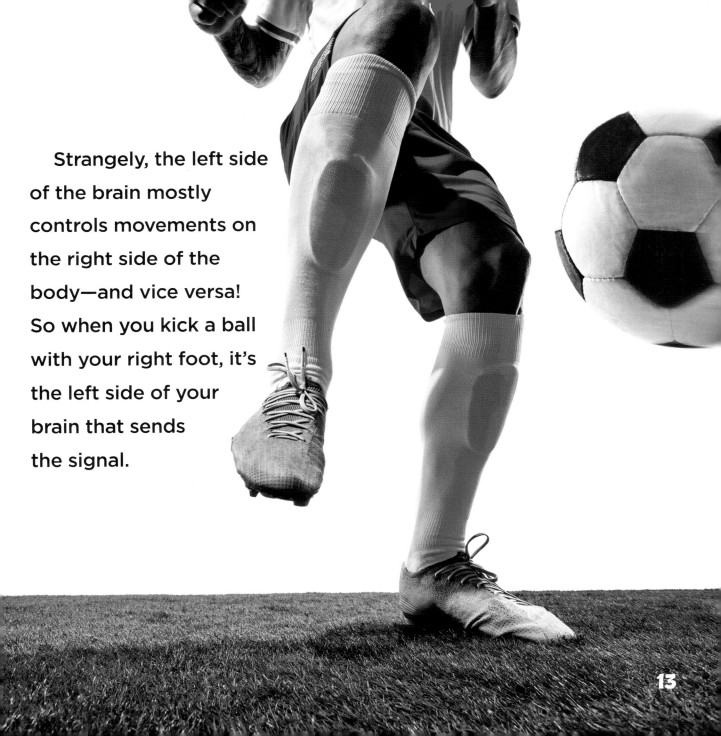

Strangely, the left side of the brain mostly controls movements on the right side of the body—and vice versa! So when you kick a ball with your right foot, it's the left side of your brain that sends the signal.

The cerebellum is like a tinier version of the cerebrum. It's the main area in your brain for movement, coordination, and balance. Your cerebellum allows you to carry a cupcake without dropping it. It also helps you sip water without spilling or throw a Frisbee to a running dog.

The brain stem is located at the base of the brain. It's about the size of an adult's thumb. Made of lots of little parts, the brain stem is responsible for breathing and other basic body functions. Without it, you wouldn't be able to blink, run, or pose for a selfie.

In addition, the brain stem helps with sleep, breathing, wakefulness, digestion, and many other functions. It controls tons of things without your having to think about them. Thanks, brain stem!

BALANCE

Like movement, balance involves many parts of the brain and body. "Balance is a complex system," says brain scientist Brad Manor. To maintain balance, your ears, eyes, muscles, and nerves all work together, each sending signals to the brain.

Your ears are one of the most critical parts of balance. Inside each of your ears is a liquid-filled **canal** dotted with tiny hair cells. When you move your head, the liquid moves the cells and **stimulates** a nerve. In less than a second, signals travel from that nerve to your brain. Then your brain tells your muscles and eyes what to do to help you stay balanced.

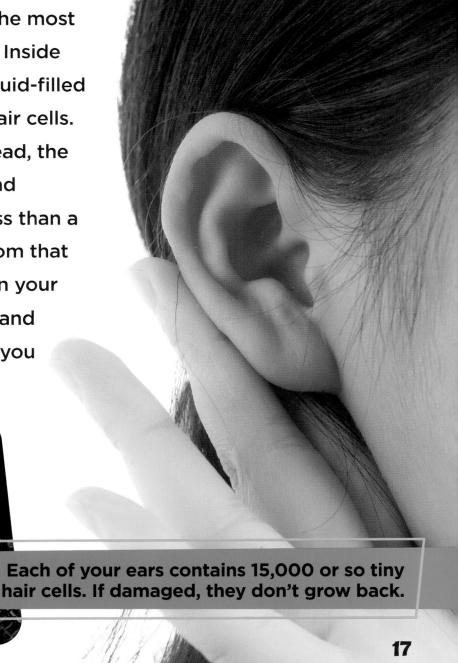

Each of your ears contains 15,000 or so tiny hair cells. If damaged, they don't grow back.

Your brain also receives signals from your eyes. It uses these signals to create images to help you see the world and your place in it. For example, each eye takes in slightly different information about an object in front of you. This helps you figure out how near or far the object is and keeps you from tripping or falling over it.

18

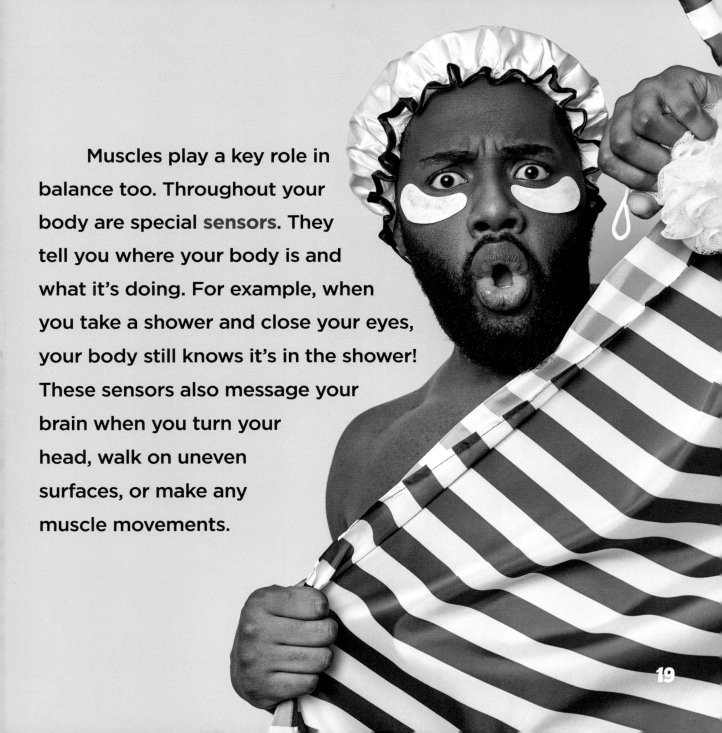

Muscles play a key role in balance too. Throughout your body are special **sensors**. They tell you where your body is and what it's doing. For example, when you take a shower and close your eyes, your body still knows it's in the shower! These sensors also message your brain when you turn your head, walk on uneven surfaces, or make any muscle movements.

OFF BALANCE

Some people, like high-wire walkers, have great balance. Others lose their ability to balance, sometimes completely. In 2004, a woman developed a condition called vertigo (VUHR-tih-goh). It was an extreme case. She was so dizzy she couldn't stand, walk, or even open her eyes. Doctors found an issue in her cerebellum. By treating it, they cured her vertigo.

Vertigo can also be caused by less serious problems like an ear infection or virus.

As people age, they also can lose their balance. The hair cells in their ears can die off, making it easier to fall. Eyesight can fail and muscles weaken. Experts say people who exercise have a better chance of keeping their brains and bodies healthy. So get moving!

Astronauts in space may develop severe vertigo. Why? Without gravity, the fluid in their ears sloshes around, stimulating their hair cells.

BRAIN GAMES

Put on some sneakers. Next, balance on your right foot. While standing on one foot, take off your left sneaker. Then put it back on without losing your balance! Do the same thing while standing on your left foot.

Now, grab a broom and go outside. Try to balance the handle of the broom on your right index finger and talk at the same time. Do the same thing while balancing the broom on your left finger.

◇ Was it harder to balance on one side or the other? Why do you think that is?

GLOSSARY

brain stem (BRAYN STEHM) the part of the brain that controls essential actions, like breathing and swallowing

canal (kuh-NAL) a round duct containing fluid

cerebellum (ser-uh-BEH-luhm) the part of the brain that controls balance and coordination

cerebrum (suh-REE-bruhm) the part of the brain that forms thoughts

chemical (KEH-muh-kuhl) a natural substance that helps the body function

condition (kuhn-DIH-shuhn) general health; shape

digestion (dih-JES-chuhn) the process by which food is broken down within the body and turned into energy

electrical (i-LEK-truh-kuhl) related to the flow of electricity, a form of energy

feat (FEET) an act or achievement that takes courage, skill, or strength

nerves (NUHRVS) bundles of fibers that pass signals between the brain, spinal cord, or other parts of the body

organ (OR-guhn) a body part that does a particular job

sensors (SEN-suhrz) things that pick up or measure something, such as movement

stimulates (STIM-yuh-layts) raises levels of activity of something in the body

synapses (SIH-nap-suhs) gaps between neurons where nerve impulses, or signals, travel

23

FiND OUT MORE

Books

Mason, Paul. *Your Mind-Bending Brain and Networking Nervous System*. New York, NY: Crabtree Publishing, 2016.

Silver, Donald M., and Patricia J. Wynne. *My First Book About the Brain*. Mineola, NY: Dover Publications, 2013.

Simon, Seymour. *Brain: Our Nervous System*. New York, NY: HarperCollins, 2006.

Websites

American Museum of Natural History: Brain Introduction
https://www.amnh.org/exhibitions/brain-the-inside-story/brain-introduction

The Franklin Institute: Your Brain
https://www.fi.edu/your-brain/interactives

KidsHealth: Balance Disorders
https://kidshealth.org/LurieChildrens/en/parents/balance-disorders.html?ref=search

INDEX

ABOUT THE AUTHOR

Joyce Markovics has written hundreds of books for kids. She's fascinated by the human brain and all its complexities. She would like to dedicate this book to Peter Markovics, who enjoys moving all over New York City as a means of staying balanced.